The Worlds Within

How Environments Shape the Developing Child

Freudian Trips

Copyright Page

Disclaimer

The views and opinions expressed in this book are those of the author(s) and do not necessarily reflect the official policy or position of any other agency, organization, employer, or company. The contents of this book are for informational and educational purposes only and are not intended to serve as professional advice, diagnosis, or treatment.

The information provided in this book is believed to be accurate and reliable as of the date of publication. However, it may include some errors or inaccuracies, and no warranty or guarantee is provided regarding the accuracy, timeliness, or applicability of the content.

Readers are encouraged to consult with professional philosophers, educators, or other qualified professionals where appropriate for personalized advice. The author(s) and publisher shall not be liable for any loss, damage, or harm caused or alleged to be caused, directly or indirectly, by the information or ideas contained, suggested, or referenced in this book.

By reading this book, the reader acknowledges and agrees that they are solely responsible for how they interpret and apply the information contained herein.

This book may also include references to other works, studies, and sources. These references are provided for further reading and exploration and do not imply endorsement or validation of the specific theories, viewpoints, or interpretations presented in those works.

Introduction: Beyond the Individual – Why Environment Matters

Imagine you have two rose bushes with the exact same seeds. You plant one in rich soil with plenty of sunlight and water. You plant the other in hard, dry ground with limited sun. Can you guess which rose bush will grow healthy and vibrant? This simple example shows that a child's development isn't just about who they are on the inside; it's deeply shaped by the world around them.

This idea might seem obvious now, but that wasn't always the case. A psychologist named Urie Bronfenbrenner changed how we think about child development. Here's his story and why it matters.

The Man Who Saw the Big Picture: Urie Bronfenbrenner

Urie Bronfenbrenner was born in Russia in 1917. When he was six, his family moved to the United States. As a young man, he studied both music and psychology. This love of patterns helped him see the big picture when studying children. After serving in the U.S. Army during World War II, he became a professor and dedicated his life to understanding how to support healthy child development.

Before Bronfenbrenner: The Child in a Bubble

In Bronfenbrenner's time, many psychologists focused on the child in isolation. They studied things like intelligence or personality as if these were set in stone, separate from outside forces. Think of scientists in a lab, carefully controlling experiments. This helped them understand parts of development, but it was missing something.

A New Way of Thinking: It's the System!

Bronfenbrenner realized that kids couldn't be studied like objects in a lab. Their families, schools, neighborhoods, and even their country's laws all played a part in shaping who they became. He saw these forces not as separate, but as connected and interacting layers.

He also realized that some of these forces were directly felt by the child, while others exerted a more hidden influence. Think of how a parent's tough day at work can make bedtime more stressful, even if the child didn't see the workplace struggles.

Why This Matters

Bronfenbrenner's ideas were revolutionary because they provided a framework. This framework allowed us to understand problems children face and see the points where we could make a difference. It showed that solutions couldn't just be about the child alone, but about improving the whole system around them.

Up Next...

Now that you understand the big idea, we're ready to dive into the layers of Bronfenbrenner's world, starting with the child's immediate surroundings!

Chapter 1: Mapping a Child's World

Think of a child as a tiny island. Islands aren't isolated – they're shaped by the waters around them, the weather patterns, and even distant shores. Urie Bronfenbrenner believed something similar was true for children. To really understand them, we need a map of all the forces that shape their lives.

Bronfenbrenner's Map: Layers of Influence

Bronfenbrenner's "map" of development has several layers. We'll imagine them like circles expanding outward, with the child at the very center.

- **Microsystem: Home Base**
- This is a child's most immediate world: family, school, friends, and neighborhood. Think of the people they see every day and the places they spend the most time.
- Example: A loving family creates a positive microsystem vs. one with conflict.

- **Mesosystem: Connections Count**
- This is where parts of the microsystem meet. Parent-teacher conferences, friendships between neighborhood kids, even how your parents' work affects family life – those are all the mesosystem in action.
- Example: A negative mesosystem would be a child with a great school but a chaotic home life. Support from one area can't fully make up for struggles in another.
- **Exosystem: The Influences You Don't See**
- This layer is where the child doesn't have direct contact, but it still affects them. Think of it like the currents around the island, shaping the shoreline.
- Examples: Parent's workplace stress, economic downturns, local availability of things like parks or healthcare all belong here.
- **Macrosystem: The Big Picture**
- This is the broadest layer – the island's "climate zone." It includes the laws, values, and customs of the child's culture.
- Examples: A society that views children as important vs. one that doesn't, the focus on individualism vs. community, religious beliefs – these are like the overall weather patterns affecting the child.
- **Chronosystem: The Power of Time**
- This layer cuts across all the others. It's about how events and changes over time shape a child's path. Think of it like storms reshaping the island.
- Examples: A family moving, a parent losing a job, historical events, even changes in technology. The **when** something happens is part of its impact.

The Ever-Changing Map

Picture those nested circles – they're not set in stone! Experiences move a child between the layers. A kid visiting a sick grandparent has a glimpse into the exosystem world of hospitals. The world also shifts around them – a new baby in the family changes everything.

Why This Map Matters

Bronfenbrenner's map helps us understand that a child's development isn't just about their own effort. It shows us where to look for strengths and where a child might need extra support.

Up Next...

Now that you have the big picture, we'll zoom in on the microsystem, the heart of a child's daily life!

Chapter 2: Home, School, and the Playground: Where Development Takes Root

Remember Bronfenbrenner's island? The microsystem is the island itself – the ground a child stands on every day. It's where the most powerful, direct influences on their development come from. Let's take a walk around this island and see what makes it so important.

Family: The Heart of the Island

For most kids, family is the absolute core of their microsystem. Whether it's parents, siblings, grandparents, or close family friends – it's the people providing love, care, and setting the first rules.

Think of family like the soil the child's planted in. Rich, nurturing soil helps a plant thrive, while harsh soil makes it harder. Here's what matters:

- **Warmth vs. Conflict:** Does the child feel safe and loved or is there a lot of tension or neglect?

- **Parenting Styles:** Are parents strict, permissive, or finding that middle ground? Different styles lead to different outcomes for kids.
- **Stability:** Are there big changes like divorce, or frequent moves, or is their family life a strong, predictable base?

School: The Learning Lab

School is where kids officially step out into the broader world. It's more than just tests and homework; it shapes how kids think, make friends, and see themselves.

- **The Teacher Factor:** Just like families, the warmth and support of a teacher matters enormously! A good teacher becomes like a second nurturing parent figure.
- **Classroom Climate:** Is the classroom organized and calm, or chaotic? Does the child feel like they belong, or like an outsider?
- **Friendships:** Peer relationships are formed at school, teaching kids about cooperation, dealing with conflict, and who they are outside their family.

Neighborhood and Community: The Wider Village

The island has its own ecosystem. This includes:

- **Physical Safety:** Are there safe places to play, or do kids feel worried about danger in their neighborhood?
- **Resources:** Parks, libraries, community centers... these are like extra fertilizer for healthy development. A lack of them makes it harder.

- **Sense of Community:** Does the child feel they belong, that neighbors care, or are they surrounded by strangers?

It's Not Just About One Part

The microsystem's power isn't about any one part being perfect. It's how they all fit together. A rough home life can be partly soothed by an amazing teacher. A lack of neighborhood resources can be balanced somewhat by a strong, loving family.

Up Next...

We've seen how powerful those closest circles around the child are. But remember, they don't exist in a bubble! Next, we'll see how those connections between the parts of the microsystem make all the difference.

Chapter 3: Building Bridges: When the Child's Worlds Collide

Imagine a child's microsystem like a bunch of tiny islands: there's the family island, the school island, maybe a sports team island, and so on. The mesosystem is all about the bridges built between those islands. When those bridges are strong, the child can move between their worlds smoothly. Weak or broken bridges? That's when things get stormy.

The Parent-Teacher Connection: A Major Bridge

Think about parent-teacher conferences, but that's just the start. Does the parent feel comfortable going to the school? Does the teacher understand the kid's home life? If there's a problem, do they work together as a team or get stuck blaming each other?

Here's a real-life example of why this bridge matters:

- **Scenario A:** A child is acting out in class. The teacher and parents join forces, share concerns, and realize

the child is stressed due to a new sibling at home.
They find solutions together.

- **Scenario B:** The same thing happens. But the teacher blames the parents, the parents get defensive...now the child is in trouble at both home AND school, and the real reason is missed.

When Neighborhoods Spill into School

Remember that a child's neighborhood is part of their island world too. It shapes them!

- **Positive Example:** A safe, friendly neighborhood where kids play together might mean they head to school feeling happy and ready to connect with classmates.
- **Challenging Example:** A child who feels unsafe or isolated in their neighborhood might bring those worries to school, making it harder to focus and learn.

The Web, Not Just Lines

The mesosystem isn't about one-to-one connections. Imagine a spiderweb! A supportive friend group can bridge a difficult home life. A community center can connect a family to resources, which helps at school too.

Why Strong Bridges Matter

Here's the thing: every child experiences bumps in the road. It's part of growing up! But a strong mesosystem makes those bumps easier to handle. Here's why:

- **Consistency:** When adults across a kid's life agree on rules and expectations, the child knows what to do. It provides a sense of security.
- **Problem-solving:** Kids can't fix everything themselves. United adults can tackle a bullying issue, a learning difficulty, or support needed outside of school.
- **A Child's Voice:** When the different parts of a child's life 'talk' to each other, the child feels understood. This helps them build trust and advocate for themselves.

Up Next...

We've seen the power of direct connections. But remember, Bronfenbrenner's map has even wider layers! Next up, we explore how forces a child never even sees can still shape their path.

Chapter 4: Invisible Currents: How the World Shapes a Child from Afar

Remember our island analogy? The exosystem is like ocean currents the island dweller doesn't directly touch, yet those currents still change the shoreline over time. In child development, these 'currents' are things the child doesn't experience first-hand but have a ripple effect on their lives.

The Workplace Connection

Most kids will never see inside their parent's office or factory. But what happens there matters a lot!

- **Stressful Job, Stressed Parent:** A parent with long hours, little control over their schedule, or a mean boss can come home exhausted and short-tempered. Even if it's not about the child, it affects them.
- **Supportive Work, Strong Family:** Flexible hours, decent pay, and a parent who enjoys their work can mean more time and positive energy for family life.

- **Losing a Job:** This isn't just about money; it's the stress and uncertainty that spills over into a child's life, even if they don't fully understand why.

The Invisible Hand of Government

Laws and public policies may seem far away from a child's daily life, but they ripple down into the family and neighborhood. Think of things like:

- **Family Support:** Are there policies that help parents with childcare costs or time off for sick kids? Less financial stress = a calmer household for the child.
- **Community Resources:** Public libraries, parks, and after-school programs enrich a child's world. A lack of them limits opportunities.
- **School Funding:** Does the child's school have enough resources, up-to-date textbooks, and well-paid teachers? All of this translates into the child's classroom experience.

The Media's Hidden Power

TV shows, social media, video games...these aren't a part of the child's real-life interactions, but they shape how kids see the world. Think of it like the air our island dweller breathes:

- **Positive Influence?** Educational shows can teach skills; inspirational characters serve as role models.
- **Negative Influence?** Constant violence or unrealistic body images can lead to aggression or self-esteem issues.

- **The Time Factor:** Too much screen time takes away from real-world interaction, affecting social skills and development

Why the Exosystem is Tricky

A child can't directly change their parent's job situation or fix bad laws. This layer can feel frustrating because it highlights issues beyond a single family's control. But, awareness is powerful! It helps us understand:

- **Sources of Stress:** A child acting out in school might not be a 'bad kid', but be reacting to stress in their exosystem.
- **Advocacy:** Understanding this layer makes us better voters and community members as we push for policies that support children and families.

Up Next...

We've explored a layer with invisible yet powerful influences. But, there's an even broader layer shaping a child – the very culture they live in!

Chapter 5: The Climate Zone: How Big Ideas Shape a Child's World

Think of the island we've been talking about. Now imagine it in different parts of the globe: a tropical island, a rocky one in the far north, or a crowded city island. The climate zone changes EVERYTHING about how life on that island works. The macrosystem is like that climate zone for child development.

Laws and Policies: Setting the Rules of the Game

Every society has rules about how children are treated, both formal laws and unspoken ones. Here are a few examples of how this plays out:

- **Child Labor:** In some countries, it's normal for kids to work long hours in dangerous jobs. In others, laws protect childhood as a time for learning and play.
- **Discipline:** Some cultures see spanking as acceptable, while others have laws against it. This shapes how adults behave towards children.

- **Children's Rights:** Are children seen as having their own voice, or just as obeying adults? This impacts everything from family dynamics to what's expected at school.

The Power of Beliefs

Beyond written laws, a culture's mindset about children deeply affects all the inner layers of the system. Think about these questions:

- **Individual vs. Community:** Does the culture emphasize individual success, or raising kids who contribute to the group? This shapes how competition vs. cooperation is handled at school and among peers.
- **View of Childhood:** Is childhood seen as a time to be protected, or a time for kids to quickly take on adult roles? This changes what's considered the "right" pace of growing up.
- **What's Valued:** Does the culture emphasize academic success, artistic talent, athletic strength, or something different? What skill a child excels in will matter more if their culture prizes it.

Looking Across Cultures

Comparing different countries shows how the macrosystem isn't about right or wrong, it's about fit:

- **Strictness:** Some cultures might seem very harsh to outsiders, but children raised in them feel secure knowing what's expected. Change that expectation suddenly, and the system breaks down.

- **Pace of Life:** In some cultures, kids have more independence early on; in others, they're very sheltered. There isn't a single 'best' way; kids adapt to their climate zone.

Why This Matters

The macrosystem is easy to miss because it feels normal to us. But understanding it helps us:

- **Avoid Judgement:** A child acting differently from what we expect might not be "bad," they're just from a different climate zone.
- **Question Our Assumptions:** Are there outdated beliefs about children limiting how we support them?
- **Be a Force for Change:** Seeing how laws and attitudes elsewhere support kids well can inspire us to advocate for change in our own society.

Up Next...

We've covered a lot of ground, but there's one layer left! Remember, development isn't static – time shapes everything a child experiences.

Chapter 6: Time Changes Everything: When a Moment Becomes a Milestone

Imagine a plant. Giving it the same amount of water works if you do it consistently. But sudden downpours, then long droughts, will damage it! The chronosystem is about how the timing of things greatly impacts a child's path.

Consistency Matters

Kids love routines not because they're boring, but because predictability feels safe! Think about:

- **Everyday Routines:** Regular meal times and bedtimes help a child's body and mind feel secure. Chaotic schedules cause stress, even if the total amount of care is the same.
- **Rules and Expectations:** If parents or teachers change the rules unpredictably, it's confusing and frustrating. Consistency helps kids learn self-control and what's right.

When Major Events Shake Things Up

Big life changes can have a ripple effect, depending on when they happen in a child's development.

- **Moving Cities:** Upsetting for any kid, but a young child might adapt easier than a teen who loses her friend circle at a crucial time.
- **Family Changes:** A new sibling is a joy, but also stressful. Its impact depends on whether the child already feels secure, or if other things in their life are unstable too.
- **National or World Events:** Think about how a child old enough to understand news about a war or disaster might be deeply affected, while a very young child would only sense the stress of adults around them.

Technology: A New Kind of Timeline

Our island dweller has a calendar previous generations didn't: the pace of technology!

- **Young Kids:** Too much screen time too early can affect attention and social development. Their brains are wired for real-world interaction first!
- **Teens:** The explosion of social media is a whole new landscape for friendships, bullying, and anxieties that previous generations didn't face the same way.
- **The Constant Update:** The world changes and updates faster than ever. This can create pressure to keep up, or anxiety about the future.

Why Timing Isn't Destiny

The chronosystem might seem scary – what if one bad event messes up a kid's path forever? Here's the good news:

- **Resilience:** Kids are amazingly adaptable. Yes, timing matters, but support systems in the other layers can soften the blow.
- **It's Never Too Late:** Did a child have a tough start? Positive experiences later on still have immense power for healing and rerouting their path.
- **The Long View:** We don't just help a child for today, but for who they'll be in ten years. A rough patch now doesn't define a whole life.

Up Next...

We've covered a lot! It's time to revisit how using Bronfenbrenner's model can change how we see the world, and how we help kids thrive within it.

Chapter 7: Beyond the Textbook: Using the Map to Make a Difference

Bronfenbrenner's theory isn't meant to just live in a book. It's a tool! Think of it like a set of special glasses, letting us see the hidden forces shaping a child's life. This helps us understand problems better and find solutions that truly work.

Case Studies: Seeing the System in Action

Let's look at two scenarios kids might face. Bronfenbrenner's model helps us go deeper than just labeling the child:

- **Scenario A: The Struggling Student** A child fails tests, disrupts class. Old-school response: blame the kid, maybe label them as lazy or having a problem.
- **Bronfenbrenner Lens:** We look across systems – Is something chaotic at home (microsystem)? Do they feel excluded at school (mesosystem)? Is there a cultural mismatch between home and school values (macrosystem)? Understanding the cause leads to better support.

- **Scenario B: The Anxious Child** A child's worries are
  out of proportion, keeping them from making friends
  or enjoying school.
- **Bronfenbrenner Lens:** Is there an undiagnosed
  learning issue leading to low self-esteem
  (microsystem)? Are their parents also very anxious
  (exosystem)? Does media fuel fears about the world
  (exosystem)? Pinpointing the main source helps with
  the right treatment.

Where the Theory Makes a Difference

Let's zoom out to see how this way of thinking shapes entire
fields that work with kids:

- **Schools:** It's not just about the classroom. Strong
  parent connections (mesosystem), policies that
  support all families (macrosystem), and awareness of
  how timing of events impacts kids (chronosystem)
  create a more successful school.
- **Social Work:** Helping a family in crisis isn't just about
  direct aid. Understanding the job loss (exosystem),
  community resources (mesosystem), and the long-
  term impact of this stressful time (chronosystem)
  leads to support that prevents deeper problems.
- **Healthcare:** Doctors and nurses who understand that
  a child's fears aren't just 'kid stuff' but tied to their
  whole environment build better trust. This is true for
  physical and mental health.
- **Policy Makers:** Laws about child labor, early
  childhood education, etc., shouldn't be debated in a
  vacuum. The macrosystem perspective shows the

ripple effects of these choices on a whole generation of kids.

Risk and Resilience: The Power of the Whole Map

One of the most powerful things Bronfenbrenner's model highlights is that kids aren't doomed by a single bad circumstance.

* **Risk Factors:** Think of these like weights on a child's island. Poverty, family conflict, lack of resources...each adds more strain.
* **Protective Factors:** These are like strong tree roots on the island! Loving adults, a supportive school, even a child's own inner strength counterbalance the risk factors.
* **It's the Balance:** A child with many risk factors CAN thrive if we shore up the protective factors in their environment.

Up Next...

Bronfenbrenner's work sparked a revolution in how we think about kids. But its true legacy lies in the future...how will YOU use this understanding?

Chapter 8: The Ripple Effects: Where We've Been, and Where We're Going

Urie Bronfenbrenner wasn't just a scientist in a lab – he wanted to create a better world for kids. Looking back, it's clear he succeeded. His focus on the whole system around a child revolutionized how we think.

Before and After: What Changed

Here's a simple way to understand Bronfenbrenner's impact:

- **Before:** The focus was on the individual child. Strengths or problems were seen as being inside the kid. The solution? Focus on fixing the child themselves.
- **After:** We understand that kids are embedded in a system. A 'problem child' might have a perfectly healthy inner self, but be battling difficult circumstances. Solutions involve changing the environment, not just the child.

Fair Criticisms

Like any theory, Bronfenbrenner's has been refined over time.
Here are some points where people have pushed it further:

- **Child's Active Role:** The original model could make a
  kid seem passive. But, kids aren't just shaped by their
  environment, they shape it! A bubbly kid melts a
  grumpy parent; a curious kid seeks out good teachers.
- **Culture:** Early versions could be interpreted as "one
  size fits all." There's increased sensitivity now to how
  different cultures shape all the layers, and how the
  theory must adapt across the globe.
- **Power:** Who benefits from the status quo of the
  macrosystem? Bronfenbrenner's work inspires us to
  question systems that may claim to help children, but
  actually uphold inequalities.

The Future: Questions that Excite Us

Bronfenbrenner's system provides a framework for endless
questions relevant to today's world:

- **The Brain and the System:** How do early
  experiences change the developing brain? This links
  biology and environment.
- **Technology's Impact:** The chronosystem looks very
  different with social media, AI...what are the long-term
  effects on development?
- **Global & Local:** How does a world crisis trickle down
  to a child's neighborhood? How can local support
  systems counterbalance global problems?
- **A Seat at the Table:** How can kids THEMSELVES use
  this model to advocate for their needs?

Bronfenbrenner's True Legacy

It's not about a diagram memorized for an exam. Bronfenbrenner gave us all a way of seeing. Whether you're a parent, teacher, policy maker, or just someone who cares about the next generation, this theory asks us:

- **Where to Look:** Faced with a child's struggle, don't rush to blame. Instead, map their world to uncover what's holding them back.
- **Where to Act:** Solutions aren't one-size-fits-all. We must strengthen the system around a child, layer by layer.
- **Why Hope Matters:** Kids are amazingly resilient. Even if they've faced challenges, improving their environment changes their trajectory. It's never too late.

Conclusion: The Power of Seeing the Whole Picture

We've traveled from a single island – your individual child – out to the currents, climate, and changing tides that shape their life. It may feel overwhelming at times, but Bronfenbrenner's theory is ultimately about hope and possibility.

Why This Matters

Understanding child development through the lens of systems helps us understand ourselves better too:

- **Parents:** You aren't alone! A difficult day at work may have lingering effects you don't even realize. But seeking community support, advocating for family-friendly policies...those are positive ripples in your child's system.
- **Teachers:** It's more than your classroom. Connecting with parents, understanding cultural backgrounds of kids, and being aware of the 'invisible' stuff they carry in is part of your profound impact.

- **Everyone Else:** Do you volunteer with kids? Vote in local elections? Even interact with a grumpy child at the grocery store? You are a tiny part of their system. Every bit of kindness, patience, and support adds up.

Systems Thinking for a Better World

Bronfenbrenner's biggest gift is a way of thinking. Old approaches kept hitting walls because they only saw part of the picture. Whether you're raising your own kids, involved in their lives professionally, or just want to make society better, remember:

- **Problems Have Roots:** Quick fixes don't work. Understanding the 'why' behind a child's struggles leads to the right solutions.
- **Small Changes Matter:** Can't change the whole macrosystem today? Tutor a child, befriend a stressed parent, start a conversation that challenges outdated views.
- **The Long Game:** The child in front of you matters, but so does the future adult they'll become. Everything we do to improve their environment now pays off for years to come.

One Last Look at the Island

Imagine that kid on their island. We can't control all the winds and currents. Some challenges will always be part of life. But because of Bronfenbrenner, we know to build stronger bridges, plant shelter from the storms, and teach them to navigate.

Their island isn't isolated. We're all part of ensuring it isn't a lonely place, but one rich with opportunity and support for them to truly thrive.

About Freudian Trips

Welcome to Freudian Trips, your dedicated platform for diving deep into the world of psychology. We are more than just a YouTube channel or a book publisher. We are a beacon of enlightenment, making complex psychological concepts accessible and engaging for all.

Our YouTube channel is a rich repository of psychology made simple. We take the profound and often complex ideas from the world of psychology and break them down into digestible, easy-to-understand content. From the foundational theories of Freud to the cognitive insights of Piaget, we cover a broad spectrum of psychological schools and thoughts, making psychology accessible to everyone, regardless of their background or prior knowledge.

As a book publisher, we take the same approach, transforming intricate psychological theories into comprehensible narratives. Our books are not just collections of words, but vessels of wisdom that make psychology approachable and relatable. We believe that psychology should not be confined to academic circles, but should be available to all who seek to understand the human mind and behavior.

At Freudian Trips, we believe in the power of curiosity and the pursuit of knowledge. We are here to stoke the fires of your curiosity, to guide you on your intellectual journey, and to help you navigate the fascinating world of psychology.

If you are someone who is not afraid to question, to explore, and to learn, then you are in the right place. Join us on this journey of exploration, as we make psychology easy to understand, one concept at a time.

Be sure to visit our Youtube channel at:
www.freudiantrips.com/youtube

You can also visit us on the web at www.freudiantrips.com

Welcome to The Freudian Trip community. Stay curious. Stay enlightened.